Observable Acts

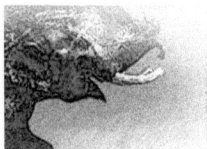

Observable Acts

A Collection of Poetry

Kevin Barger

Contents

Observable Act #1

An observable act
A glance
Scattered an eternity
He played guitar
I played with words
Our only connection
An empty microphone

Public Service Announcement

This is a public service announcement to all of my future
       lovers
Come prepared
Because I may not look like much
But I have a heart that flings fire from fingernails
Rests stars on eyelashes
And if gone unchecked
Has the potential to bring civilization down to its knees

But don't let that scare you

See, I keep my heart within my mouth
My soul within my chest
And I only allow my heart to speak
When my soul says that it's okay to

So don't get offended when I tell you that I love you
Because it's not an instantaneous decision
But merely an observation
Through hollow eyes
That have looked into the core of your soul
And have found a light there
That they wish to make brighter

Even though you try to hide it with nervous laughter

But don't let that scare you either

And don't try to be something that you're not
Because I'll see right through you

And chances are I'll find no fault
Within your faults
So lay them on the line
And don't make me waste time
Trying to separate your lies
From mine
Because I'm not going to promise I won't lie to you
When you ask me to:

"No, your messy house doesn't bother me."

"I think your cat is so intelligent."

"Do I mind helping you watch your five year old nephew on
        a night that we had planned to spend together? Of
        course not! I love kids!"

But I will promise
To place my laughter within your breath
And gentleness in absurdity
And to only stay
A phone call
And a hug away
If you promise the same
And if that scares you
Then stay at home
And lock your door
And I'll be sitting here on my bedroom floor
Writing poetry in a leather bound journal
Wondering why you haven't found me yet
And I'll grow more cynical the older I get

Until eventually
Life passes us both by
And as each of us take our last
Heavy breaths

We'll pause
And wonder why we never found comfort in another's smile
So bite back your fear
And stand with me

Here

And I'll bring you back to your regularly scheduled program

Observable Act # 2

A touch
Lit the sky behind my eyes
I said I love you
He said nothing
Falls only hurt at the end

Impossible Poetry

If I knew how
I would write for you a poem
While sitting in a red leather chair
At a mahogany desk
In my own private library filled with books.

I would take a feather quill
In my hand
And pen the most beautiful images
Add a dash of metaphor and simile
Craft sneaky rhymes that
Hide between the lines on yellow parchment paper.

When I was through
I would take a walk
Down cobblestone streets
With a top hat
And a cane
And people would whisper as they saw me pass
Saying there goes the next
Whitman, Tennyson, Parker, or Poe.

And when I made it to your front door
I would hand you my new creation
And you would read it
And smile
And finally say:

I love you.

But I don't know how to write that poem.

The Sign at the Church

The sign at the church on the left
When I forsook your house said:

Thank you for worshiping with us.

If I had a trumpet
I would sound it like Jericho
To shatter your wall
So I could kneel at your feet
And accept whatever gratitude your religion wanted to give
        me.
Blood would seep from pores
And tears from eyes
But those aren't the bodily fluids
You are interested in.

Tomorrow I will look at the sky and pray
And I will hear your voice echo through memory:

This sin is not enough.
This sin is not enough.
This sin is not enough.

Observable Act #3

A yawn
Signaled the end
I said goodbye
He said nothing
I finally knew him

Lessons

This is a poem for all those
Who have loved
And lost
And wished to God that they had never loved at all.

I've climbed that mountain
Felt the stars at my feet
Saw the air below me
And dove head first into cold concrete.

I've been stripped bare,
Laid out shivering before a crowd of angels,
Shown a destiny that was never meant to be mine to hold,
And tasted the blood of the lamb.

Love is a lot like religion
It requires faith to grow;
Belief I had plenty of
But faith never showed.

So here's lesson one:
Never confuse two.
Faith flows in time to music.
Belief will leave you blue.
Your heart may ache for perfection,
But your soul cries out for grace.
Never settle for perfection.
Perfection will spit in your face.

Love is a realm where smoke hardly ever means fire
Instead mirrors are always in bloom.
Never miss the opportunity to look at yourself;
This is lesson two.
You may be searching for completion-
Someone whose soul may melt with yours.
Try to steer clear of that illusion.
Complete the self first
And always love it more.

I know what it's like
To lie awake each night
Listening to the sounds of your heart breaking.
Mine sounds like a frozen lake
Upon spring's first awakening.
I know what it's like also
When sleep finally comes
To dream of the one you've been longing for-
And the feeling the morning after
That you've been beaten to a pulp
Because dreams aren't reality
And reality swallows you up.

So here's lesson three:
Let the tears fall easily.
Baptize yourself in them
And never wipe them from your face.
The time will come
When you will learn
To savor their salty taste.
The more you fight the sadness

The stronger it will grow
Destroying both the body and mind-
So let the tears flow.

The hardest lesson of all
I've saved for last
It's number four:

You may always love them
But learn to shut the door.

Remember your love for all it was-
Their scent
The way your bodies fit-
But never harbor fantasies
And wipe your hands of it.
I know it's hard and trust me
I've failed at this several times.
I've tried to capture what once was-
I've used misdirection
And I've suffered for my crimes.

But this I have faith in-
Faith, not belief,
Remember lesson one-

Sometimes the path to truth is found alone.
Stand strong
And it will carry you home.

Sestina of Hope for the Used

I woke to silence
Of glittering oil
In your fantasy
I bled roses of lust
Unfelt since youth
And I shut the door

I shut the door
Sat in silence
Contemplated your chosen youth
Wished to drown him in flowing oil
I vomited out seeds of your lust
And blew away the smoke of fantasy

I sat on the edge of your fantasy
That night behind the closed door
The heartbeat of love became the punching of lust
My soul fled from fire to ice in silence
And stained itself with oil
White satin sheets have kidnapped my youth

My beauty flows deeper than the illusion of youth
I cannot be contained in its fantasy
Now unclean—I embrace the oil
And let its sweet scent flow in through the open door
I lay breathing in silence
No longer chained to lust

One night of lust
Finally destroyed my youth
Blessed with disillusioned silence
No more do I stand in fantasy
Caged by a locked door
I sing quietly—sanctified by oil

My fingers flow rainbows of oil
Forever changed by a moment of lust
They are as wise as an ancient oak door—
As gentle and cunning as youth
One small touch can unleash fantasy
Another will hold you in silence

The silence of my reflection has been shattered by oil
And I can clearly see the fantasy of betrayal and lust
No more does youth call me to open the door

Observable Act # 4

A search
Led me through my past
Into release

Lullaby

I don't want to write this poem

I was born in the middle of the night
In the middle of March
I don't remember it
But I should
I should be able to remember the smell of disinfectant
My mother's screams
The chill of the air
The warmth of the doctor's hands
And the pain of my first spanking
Like just being born was a punishable offense

I don't want to write this poem

What I do remember is third grade
Christmas time
And lying in a giant bed with three of my cousins
The smell of sweat
My oldest cousin's hands down my pants
Too much wood in the stove
A red typewriter
And thirty pairs of eyes judging me
Two weeks later when I returned to school

I don't want to write this poem

I remember playing games
Most with an element of chance
Ours was no different

If someone found out
We lost
If not
We kept playing
And we kept playing
Sometimes with two players
Sometimes three
Most of the time four
But numbers never meant much to me
What meant the most was the taste of salt
The firmness in my tiny hand
And a cloudless sky
In which an uncaring god looked down on us
Like a pedophile

I don't want to write this poem

I wish I knew what virginity felt like
I wish I could remember being pure
But what I remember is an uncircumcised penis
And wondering why it was so different
Than my own
I remember a sickening wetness in my pants
While speaking to my late grandmother
And I remember puberty
My oldest cousin calling me a fag
And not seeing him since

I don't want to write this poem
But I do want to tell this story
For the cathartic numbness to quiet
The pain of the child locked within me
And that child wants to write this poem

To be his lullaby
Not for applause
Or for scores
But for a thousand voices in a harmony of understanding
And he will sleep
And when he sleeps
He will dream
And the molestation of his childhood
The splintering of the self
The questioning
The questioning of the questioning
Will be lit with daylight
And the nightmares will fade with the darkness
Because monsters only have power if they have someplace to
        hide
And I'm sick of hiding them in closets of bitter heartbreak
I'm sick of jumping at shadows
And pipes clinking in the dark
This lullaby will be his salvation
And scary stories will vanish in the night

So hush little baby...

I've said all the words

My Grandfather's House

My grandfather's house was built on a hill overlooking the
            river.
Sunsets that stain the skies copper
Filter through windows
Masquerading as walls.
In the winter wood is fed hourly
To a massive stone fireplace
That burns until its bed time;
And even then continues to ember
Until the sun wakens from its slumber
To the opening blossoms of the cherry tree alarm clock
Kept out back and waving
To the crab apple tree
Down the hill.

My grandfather's house was built on black skin.
White flesh was never meant to meet dark tongues-
And my grandfather was never a kind man.
He is strong and sturdy.
The way oak trees are-
The way the ropes were
When my great-grandfather
Donned a white hood
And as my grandfather stood wide-eyed as a boy
Stretched rope over bark
Over flesh
Over air
And my grandfather still believes it was right.

My grandfather's house was built on a hill overlooking the
    river.
The skies are stained sanguine.
Windows masquerading as walls reflect bruised flesh
And broken necks.
In the winter the fire is fed hourly-
Crackling in a stone prison
And never allowed to die.
A sleeping sun
Is woken by blood red cherry juice
Running down the hill
To the crab apple tree
That spits its sour fruit
To rot in the lawn.

Observable Act #5

A shot
Destroyed a boy's life
I cried
And then I wrote
And then I screamed

Little Brother

Dedicated to the memory of Lawrence King, shot in his first period classroom on February 12, 2008.

I wonder if he smiled
As he pulled the trigger
Gunshot smoke filling his nostrils
As his unwanted Valentine fell to the floor
Your body crumpling in a strangely silent classroom
Your blood pooling
Blood pooling
Blood pooling
Into my veins

We are brothers with different parents
Sharing the same gene
That magnetically attracts us to other men
The blood that flows under my skin
Is the same as that which once flowed under yours
We are part of a family of strangers
And I'm sorry
I'm sorry
I'm sorry
Little brother
For we have failed you

We have grown complacent in imagined normalcy
They gave us a cable channel
And we felt equal
In a world where the phrase

That's so gay
Is thrown around in everyday conversation
To deride that which is inferior
And the word faggot is justified by those
Who claim not to be homophobic
By announcing they just use it as a term for those they don't
        like
We have failed you
When the only role models you may have had were the Fab
        Five on Queer Eye
We have failed you
When the only things on exhibit as gay culture
Are bars
Clubs
Sex
And dance music
Making us walking commercials
For breweries
Condom companies
And E dealers
We have failed you

And I'm sorry
I'm sorry
I'm sorry little brother
That the message received by your Valentine
Was that it was alright to kill
Because we don't fight back
And we're just another group to laugh at
The comedic relief in any movie without a plot

We must make that message stop

So my tongue now becomes salt
And I will lick our self-inflicted wounds
Until your killer
And his killers
Learn the real meaning of hate

And fight to combat it
With the light
Of your smile

Amen

I sit
On an uncomfortable church pew
And listen to a Southern Baptist preacher talk to me about
        sin
And how the way I walk my life will lead me straight to Hell
He quotes Romans
And Leviticus
And doesn't miss a punished jab at the Buddhists

With controlled anger I sit
And try not to shake
I should have told him Amen

Amen to all the heterosexuals
Amen to all the homosexuals
Amen to all the bisexuals
Amen to all the transsexuals
Amen to all the try sexuals
Amen to all people
Of all sexual orientation

For God is all love
And as such there is no room for hate
Yet hate brings in more money
For uncomfortable church pews
And little pamphlets proclaiming the love of "God"
For all people who happen to look exactly the same

A philosophy based solely in belief and hatred
Has no business within my bedroom

And definitely not within my pants

A philosophy based solely in belief and hatred
Has no right proclaiming who I should love

A philosophy based solely in belief and hatred
Does not create within me any shred of respect
While it condemns those who are closer to me than family
And condones those who would cause the streets to run red
          with our blood

So Amen
Amen
Amen
To all those who like me will never be afraid to love
And to be loved
Amen
To all those who are quietly faithful
But will loudly scream against unreal hate filled gods
Amen
To every bitchy queen
Who has ever stood in the face of someone who just
          shouted faggot in the middle of a crowded mall
And ripped them a new asshole
Amen
Amen
Amen
Can I get an Amen?

The difference between belief
And faith
Is that belief will only go so far
As your own personal indignation

Faith
Is much stronger
It does not write tracts
Or stand on street corners and scream about Hell
Instead it is quiet
And it listens
It watches
And it waits
It flows and
Perhaps it changes over time

I should have said this and a lot more
But my tongue sticks like peanut butter to the roof of my
          mouth
And I hate the taste

Countdown

1

One night
One night was all I needed with him
As he shot me a look from across the room
That wrapped a lightning bolt
Around my neck
And pulled me forward
Like in those old timey cartoons
He breathed a smile
And kissed me
And suddenly I'm wrapped up in fantasy
And I don't know if it was the beer
Or the moonlight
But whatever it is that makes me
Me
Left my body
Allowing room for a carnal animal to take over

And as the stars winked through his bedroom window
One
And one
Became two

2

Two days later
He says:
I probably should have told you this sooner
But my ex was HIV positive

And seeing the look of shock in my eyes
He assures me that he's negative
And that they were extremely careful
But my right shoulder angel
And my left shoulder devil
Have been replaced
By fear
And guilt
And I have to wonder how careful they could have been
When I don't even know his middle name
But as we played on the fairground of hormones
We didn't even use a fucking condom

But I file all this into shit that I will deal with later
Assure him that I'm negative too
And as long as he knows he's clean
I don't have a problem
But I decide in the back of my mind
That I will never contact him again
And pull out the later file
On day three

3

Three months
Three goddamn months
Before this window period is over
And I can go get tested
To see if after this trimester
I'm going to give birth
To an Antichrist that is going to wage
Armageddon within my veins
And that thought strikes me funny

Because I'm not even Christian
But right now I'm praying to whatever god that will listen
As my world devolves into clichés
Clocks tick backward
Footsteps become heavier and
I begin meditation to cleanse my mind of the fear
And somehow
I go from hazy HIV status
To Buddhist philosophy
In 3.5 seconds
As I start telling tables that they don't exist
And I don't either, really

Because we're all just a sum of our parts
And those parts of sum of theirs
And so on
And so forth
Until eventually
Everything devolves into a huge pile of nothingness
And then I decide that since walls also don't exist
I should be able to move through them
Become a super hero
HIV man
High Vs all around!

But I'm not a super hero
Just a son scared shitless
That a simple symbol used for addition: +
Will bend its arms and
Become my own personal 卐

And finally
The clocks begin ticking again

And I make an appointment to the clinic
Sit in a sterilized room
Cut the nurse's lecture on safe sex short
And become more afraid of a needle
Than I have been since I was four

4

Four hours later
The results are in
And the countdown begins:

5

4

3

2

...

Beauty

You were there last night
Dancing to music unheard
Concentrating on the flash of lights
Swaying shirtless your naked torso enhanced by crystals of
        sweat
Moving down lean muscle and gathering into the fraying
        denim of your waistband.

You had let the vibrations take over
Sound moved your body
Head unaware
Blissfully unaware.
This was your time to forget and the alcohol had permeated
        deep into your soul
Glossing over the stains hidden there since—

NO! Dance!

Everyone wanted you
Everyone wants you
Wants to be you
You are a god here tonight and every movement you make
        screams:

I love you baby,
I love you

Scenery changes and you are there again in the doorway
        holding the left arm of a yellow teddy bear missing
        one eye—mother arguing with boyfriend words
        shrill and angry—anger? No, fear—fearful tears
        running down cheekbones—mascara running rivers
        of oil

Suddenly a tackle—mother laying on newly vacuumed
        carpet—a flash of silver then a gun pointed
        underneath her throat—your voice rises in a
        scream—a cry—her voice gets softer:

I love you baby,
I love you

And you're not sure who she's talking to

A moment of indecision and morality takes hold—he stands
        and she runs—picking you up and you watch over
        her bruised shoulder as he sits on the bed—gun in
        his hand as he watches the opposite wall

I love you baby
I love you

Now another heartbeat and everything slows—his hand
        lifts—barrel pointed to temple—a ghost screams
        and a rose blooms

NO!
Dance to forget!

Now another beauty and you flow together
Sweat beads mingle and you are one
This will be your conquest tonight
Another faceless attractive stranger
Anything to forget old demons

Numbness is your friend

Dance to forget
Dance to forget
Dance to forget

Observable Act #6

A dream
Showed me whispers of what could be
I awoke
Moaning

One Night

Tonight is yours
Starlight caresses our molten forms
As sweat beads dangle from hair strands
Contemplate their existence
And jump
Free fall onto flesh
Writhing with pleasure
Then roll down to their ultimate destiny
In the sanctity of your sheets
Which feel strange
But familiar
To my naked skin

Guarded whispers escape tongues
Filling the air with words sweet and foreign
That intermingle with our combined aroma and
Set free trapped souls
Caged by passions unheeded

You think of he
I of another
And we become each other's fantasy
As the moon guides the
Ebb
And flow
Of our embrace

Soft words are eventually taken hostage by louder moans
Animalistic in their desire
To be heard over the fatal finger of daybreak

And then

You lie on your back
I on your arm
And sleep nudges me awake
To say goodbye and leave
To forget your name
But never your face

Focus

Focus on me now
Focus your touch on porous flesh
Until eruption breaks like a metaphor
Let appendages intertwine into knots
Until I can't figure out where I stop
And you begin.
Let pleasure seep through the darkness

Because that's what you're here for
Right?
For the numbing effect of alcohol
To be overshadowed
By the numbness of a stranger's bed
For the emptiness which can only come from
R----R----R---Release

But focus on me now
Slide your heavy hand up calf
Then thigh
Up stomach
Then chest
Then higher
Then higher
Then higher

Because God is up there somewhere
And if you reach far enough
Maybe you could just
Touch

But focus on me now
Let lips touch anything but lips
Because a kiss would be too personal
Just like my name or
Your real one

Focus on me now
And I'll focus on you
Turning attention to the warmth of another body
In order to melt the chill of loneliness
That dragged me from bed
To bar
Then back again

I won't recognize you tomorrow
But tonight
You're my everything
And I'll lick away each drop of this sin
Until we appear clean

Observable Act #7

A moan
Brought voices to my window
I sat with each of them
And listened to their stories

Dancers

The day I died I asked Divinity
To take me back to that weeping white winter
Who danced through heart and mind with bare slender feet
And twirled gracefully among us all into her own mortality

The winter I had forgotten
Busied with immaturity
And emotion
And frigid lust
Still she danced through my self-induced sorrow and
           ignorance of love
Laughing with snow freshly painted on limbs

Divinity anticipated my request and did not think
Silently
With heavy hand
I regained life of a sort in bitter cold
So to please her I danced
Winter held in my arms
Waltzing in sweet harmony
The hollow whistle of North Wind our only music
Throughout a gaping eternity

Dementia

In Memory of Katherine

I don't know how old the memory is
But it's there on repeat:

>Today is Saturday
>Yesterday was Wednesday
>My boy Roy shot himself yesterday
>It should be in the paper
>Here's your keys

She mentions the names of people long gone
People she thinks I know
She says that Sally wants one hundred and fifty dollars
But she's not getting it
That's the truth

>There are people that come into my room
>I don't know who they are
>They're two faced
>And ready to walk out on me
>I'll miss them
>They shave my face

Her face is knowing
Nodding
Like she's imparting some secret
Something that she just can't make me understand
But it's important that I do

Today is Saturday
Yesterday was Wednesday
My boy Roy shot himself yesterday
It should be in the paper
Here's your keys

She's not upset about it
She doesn't cry like someone who just lost someone
She just mentions it
Like speaking about the weather

That black car outside
It isn't there anymore
Someone must have picked it up

Someone named James tows her car every day
And never gives it back
She wants to stop him
I think it's her way of saying
That there was something else she forgot
Another face faded
Towed away someplace
And she can't pay to get it back

It's in impound
Gone

Tom came by yesterday
I told him he doesn't work here anymore
And he left

People keep leaving
Dying, or stealing

And she keeps telling them the truth
But they don't understand
Won't understand

Her voice is gravelly
And low
And if you're not sharply focused
You'll miss it

Today is Saturday
Yesterday was Wednesday
My boy Roy shot himself yesterday
It should be in the paper
Here's your keys

Here's your keys

Here's your keys

It's lunch time now
And she wheels herself down white halls
To the dining room
Forgetting that we spoke
But she'll be back at my desk
In a couple of hours
And we'll do this again

And it'll be the first time that I've heard it

Bag Lady

She's a bag lady
Scraping food from concrete
She walks city streets
The glimmer of innocence gone from her eyes.
Catching raindrops on her tongue
She's sealed on the run
From a past she knows she can't hide.

She says, "When I be five
I be a dancer
Twirlin' under starry sky.
But I stop dancin' long ago
And now I ain't seen the stars
Fo' the glare.

When the wind blow
It be like the moon explode
But moon rocks be softer
Than my husband's fist.

I never seen this future comin'
But I gotta keep on runnin'
And hope that someday
I'll straighten out the where.

In my ol' life
I be scared like a mouse.
Hidin' in hole after hole
In that godforsaken house.
But now I'm a crow

Eatin' the roadkill off yo' city streets
But at least I can fly in the mist.

I don't want no savin'.
I save myself.
Save yo' sweet talkin'
And yo' ass kissin'
And yo' feel goodin'
Fo' someone who need it.

You got yo' job
And you got yo' house
You got yo' car
And yo' TV
And yo' spouse
But you ain't got no time.
My bags be mine.
And my mind be fine.
The only change I need

I need fo' wine."

Graffiti

He looked better behind the glass
Paint shooting from fingertips
In a pure city
With its pure rules
And creative asphyxiation.
White walls tumbled beneath each dancing movement
As he screamed silently visually
With his illegal art.

I watched each stroke
On his canvas
From my office window
Eight floors up
Cramped over keyboard
Over work
Over time
My sweat stained shirt clung to me
In an air conditioned leather chair.

At first I was appalled by his brazenness
Then curious of his intent
Then rabid with religious furor
As his message became clear.

I was baptized in each black droplet
Sanctified in each high velocity liquid collision
And ordained as he wrote his final word
And ran before the cops came.

Loosening my tie I closed the

Office door behind me
Leaving butchery in order
For sanctuary in chaos
I intoned his message
As Om:

I stood here
With paint flowing from my fingers
As a dirty artist in an impure world.
I've made my mark
Have you?

Fingernails

I am fingernails

I am eyelashes
And sweat
And bone
And gristle

I am blood
And spit
And teeth
And pustules

I am tongue
And feet
And back hair
And piss
And shit
And cum

I am nature

I am the unborn fetus in the egg
I had for breakfast
I am the tree which made the splinter
Lodged within my palm

I am air
In breath and vocal chords
I am electricity
In neurons and nerves

I am thought
And speech
And emotion

I am force
And movement
And gravity

I am

And you are

And in our shared am-ness
We represent a universe
Constantly growing
And trying its best to shine
Light in its own darkness
By creating stars
And planets
And hearts

Beating

Together

Even as we stand apart

Observable Act #8

A kiss
From new lips
Released me from his memory
And healed my scars

Spiders and the Beach

Last night I dreamt of spiders and the beach
Not the ocean
Because as I walked it just kept getting farther away
And all I could see was wet sand
Where the water had been and
Broken seashells cut my feet
As I chased it

Last night I dreamt of spiders
Of trees growing out of the sand
And massive webs stretching between them
With even larger arachnids
Each of them with your face
And I sat down and spoke with them
As moonlight danced over their threads
Turning them beautiful

I dreamt of talking to you
Conversing of things that
Neither of us can talk about yet
Like how hearts always swell before they break
Only to swell again
Until someone applies ice

I don't know if I want to be captured
Because if I allow you to feed upon me
I will feed upon you
And we will disappear into each other
Leaving only our tightly rolled husks
Dangling on silver strings

I'm as afraid of you
As I am excited about your possibilities
Like how I felt about fireworks as a child
Watching the fuse melt with wide eyes
With my hands over my ears

I'm afraid of your explosion
But I want to be touched by your sparks

I want you to set me on fire with your venom
So that the webs burn
And we have no choice but to chase the sea
No matter how much our feet bleed

At least we will leave a trail
In case we need to be rescued

Absinthe

He tastes like absinthe
An acquired taste of
Black anise and sweetness
I inhale him like cigarette smoke
Breathe in his fire
Caress his ash
And need another hit
When the last pull is done

I trace the constellations of the freckles on his back
There, Scorpio
Intense, passionate, regenerative
Here, Pisces
Reflective, intuitive, introspective
Brought together on the star map of his flesh
A tattoo drawn at birth
His is the only universe I want to exist in

His lips whisper
Dark chocolate and raspberries
Merlot and asiago
Sweet tea and mashed potatoes
He nourishes me with his smile
Heals me with his touch
Penetrates me with his stare

I have no more secrets
I am laid bare

Meteors

Tonight there is a meteor shower
And I would give all that I have
To be lying on a blanket
In some field with you
Gazing up at the stars
And wondering how far those rocks
Had traveled
Just to burn up in our atmosphere
Creating a light show
Just for the two of us

Tonight the cicadas
Are making music outside
Playing their instruments
In hope that some other beautiful bug
Will find them in the dark
And sing a song that matches their own

The drumbeat of my heart is doing the same

I want to open your eyes to my world
This wondrous world that breathes fire from the sun
That sings smoke from the fog
And cushions footsteps with leaves on trails up mountains

I want to open my eyes to yours
To feel the heat of ginger black pepper soap on my skin
To be captivated by soothing ambient music
And be wrapped in the warm softness of your comforter
As we lay on the bed

And whisper our hearts to each other

Tonight there is a meteor shower outside
And rocks are burning in our atmosphere
Having traveled millions of miles
To explode in brilliant light for our amusement

And tonight we're apart
For the second time this week-
And I am burning, too.

Thief

Maybe the time for living is now.
Maybe it's tomorrow.
Maybe it's the day after Thursday.
Whenever I feel like breathing again
Because you took my breath away
The moment that I saw you
And I don't know where you hid it.

Maybe it's behind the maple tree in your back yard.
Or underneath the rock that you use to prop your door
        open.
Or maybe
It's wherever you hid my left sock
After the first night that we slept together.
Yeah, I know it was you don't even try to say that I lost it
        because those were my favorite pair of socks!

Just like you
Have become a favorite shirt
To wrap around myself at night.
Because I get cold every time that you steal the covers.

You know the more I think about it
The more I come to the conclusion that you're a
        kleptomaniac.
And if you're not careful
People may start to come after you with weapons.

You make me
Want a dart gun
So that I could blow out the sun and say
"Look at how your eyes sparkle
In the starlight."
Because I can't wait until night.

And then of course you'd ruin it
And say, "I can't see my own eyes!"
And I'd say, "Look, I just killed the sun for you!"
And you'd say, "Who? Jesus?"
And I...
Won't have a response.
Which I often don't have
When it comes to you.
Because you steal those, too.

Traces of the goo left behind by your sticky fingers is
        everywhere
And I don't really want to wipe it away.
Partly because it's sentimental in a weird way
But mostly because I feel as if it would help the police find
        your fingerprints.
Even though it would be sort of odd having all of that black
        powder
Everywhere from my heart to my head.
So maybe I'll just lie back here with you instead
And listen to the sound of you breathing

Even though my pillow is missing!

Dear First Crush

Dear first crush:

I heard from you recently.
How your life had become a maelstrom
Of sparking neurons
That closed you off from the world
For the past six years.
I can't say it was unexpected.

Back then I thought you were the wind
Blowing fiercely behind pine trees
Leaving only the scent of soap in your wake.
I had planned to steal it.
Your soap I mean.
Yes, I was a little obsessed

Well, a lot obsessed.
But you were straight
And I was slightly curvy.
The way rainbows are curvy
And stuck glued to the earth
While you blew through me.

I promised myself that I would never write
Another poem about you.
That I would let your memory die
Like regrets should.
But your voice

Slightly altered and weary
Came at me again.
An echo
Calling me from deep sleep
Into the golden cavern of
Buried memory.

I thought about every time that you hugged me-
Embraced me momentarily-
With arms never meant for me.
I realized that I could close the door.

I wish that I could have known you then.
Not the way that I thought I did
While floating at night
Thinking about you
While you were not thinking about me.

I'm sorry for my wide eyed stares
And unwanted fingers messing up your hair.
But I swallowed my lungs every time you were near
Forcing my voice into
A mold that my misguided 18 year old self thought
Might somehow change you
Into the embodiment of my fantasy.

Tonight I sit in my car
Writing my apology letter to you.
Even though I doubt you know
How intoxicated I was by you
(I was blowing a .99).

But tomorrow the sun will rise
And like yesterday it will not
Have your face in it anymore.

Sincerely

Observable Acts

An observable act
A glance
Scattered an eternity
He played guitar
I played with words
Our only connection
An empty microphone

A touch
Lit the sky behind my eyes
I said I love you
He said nothing
Falls only hurt at the end

A yawn
Signaled the end
I said goodbye
He said nothing
I finally knew him

A search
Led me through my past
Into release

A shot
Destroyed a boy's life
I cried
And then I wrote
And then I screamed

A dream
Showed me whispers of what could be
I awoke
Moaning

A moan
Brought voices to my window
I sat with each of them
And listened to their stories

A kiss
From new lips
Released me from his memory
And healed my scars

About the Author

Kevin Barger is a performance poet, writer, and retired slam organizer based in Asheville, NC. He was instrumental in bringing slam poetry back to popularity in Asheville after its rise, fall, and subsequent misfirings in the area by helping to lay the groundwork for Poetry Slam Asheville from 2008 through 2011. He has also appeared on many other stages in and around the Carolinas including the Lake Eden Arts Festival, Lexington Avenue Arts and Fun Festival, the Individual World Poetry Slam, and Southern Fried in which he was on the first team from Asheville sent to Southern Fried in nearly a decade. Now, semi-retired from the slam scene but itching to get back on stage again, he has compiled old favorites and new material in *Observable Acts*; his first endeavor onto the published page.

Photo by Bill Rhodes

Acknowledgements

I want to extend a very hearty thank you to those who made this endeavor possible. First and foremost, thanks to Samuel Martinez and Kia Brooks for your support and feedback as I began to select pieces to include and edit.

Similarly, a huge thank you to Steven Corn who helped me more than he realizes; he has been my rock, my lover, and the inspiration of several of the poems herein-even if some of the poems inspired by him were written before meeting him.

Thank you to all of those who told me that I was a good enough poet to even attempt this: K.C. Treadway, Emily Reyes, and Andrew Procyk; without you guys telling me to go ahead and compile this, it would never have happened.

A very special thanks go to those poets I've performed with and against in slams of whom there are too many to list except for a few notables: Steve Shell, Emma Erbach, Andrew Procyk (again)-you guys were an amazing team at Southern Fried and performing and traveling with you remains one of my best memories ever. Tim Cook, Griffin Payne, and Caleb Beissert have been awesome poets and hosts of various events and performing on the same stage as you has been brilliant. Moody Black was the host of the very first slam that I ever won, and he and Kimbi the Goddess continue to inspire me with how they live their lives through their art. When I first competed against

Theresa Davis, my jaw dropped to the floor and I instantly knew that I wanted to be just like her when I grew up. I don't know if she realizes exactly how much she inspires me. There are so many more people I want to thank here, but this paragraph could turn into a book by itself.

Thanks to Jesse Davis for being there at a really delicate time for Poetry Slam Asheville and helping to keep it going so that I had an outlet for my expression. Outside of that, and more importantly, she has been an amazing friend, confidant, advice giver, pie maker, and crying shoulder. I have absolutely no idea how I could have survived these last years without her.

And last but not least, a very special thank you to my parents, Christine and Gary Barger. They have made, supported, and stood behind everything that I am. I don't even really know how to begin to thank them for everything that they are and have done. I love you guys.

Also available from
Swimming with Elephants Publications, LLC

Some of it is Muscle
Zachary Kluckman

Cunt.Bomb.
Jessica Helen Lopez

September
Katrina K Guarascio & Gina Marselle

Verbrennen
Matthew Brown

Loved Always Tomorrow
Emily Bjustrom

Of Small Children and/Other Poor Swimmers
Brian Hendrickson

To Anyone Who has Ever Loved a Writer
Nika Ann

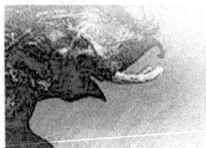

Find more titles at swimmingwithelephants.com